A Completely Unauthorized Instafreebie™ Guidebook

A Collection of Tips, Tricks, and Best Practices, With a Few Irreverent Observations

by **Dr. Robert C. Worstell**

I0485249

Also by Dr. Robert C. Worstell

Legal Shmegal

Introduction and Disclaimer

I haven't been doing Instafreebie for years, only a few months.

This book has been written with the idea of simply filling a gap.

When I started, no search would bring up anything useful about how to do anything on Instafreebie. They all said that is was a good idea, it worked for them, and how to get started.

When I first heard of this, it was (and still is) cheaper than Facebook or any other ads as a way to build a list for authors.

But don't look to see if you're going to find much content around anywhere other than how to simply set up your account. Of course, the Instafreebie support pages (at https://[1]support.instafreebie.com[2]) have a *lot* of very good starter material there. And there is a section in this book devoted to an overview of those, with links.

What you see here is my opinions of what worked for me up to this point. (Your mileage may vary – considerably.)

All these observations were blogged first, and then collected and put into this book. And that accounts for the writing styles and disjointed approach. Because I wrote things up as I stumbled over questions and problems. As I got those answered or worked them out, I then updated these.

The most important points I made several times. And you'll read them several times.

This not the finest, most tightly-edited book out there. And hopefully others will write better ones (and probably won't repeat themselves so much.) The point is to get something out *now* to fill the vacuum of data. As well as promoting the use of Instafreebie for new authors.

---

1. https://support.instafreebie.com/

2. https://support.instafreebie.com/

And the best approach to learning this book is to read it through several times. You'll get more insight as you do – and find more things to test for yourself.

Until you test what I suggest here, you won't know if it works or not. This is only what I've found that worked for me.

Where this book starts is: _now_ *what do you do?*

This book assumes you've already set up your account. This book is designed to help you get more out of Instafreebie, to get you as many subscribers and network with as many authors you can. Or at least start you in that direction.

Just today, I ran into someone who thought you could only be part of *one* giveaway at a time. This is simply fiction. I've been a part of as many as 20 giveaways at a time.

The moral of that story is to try and test everything for yourself. Especially what is in this book.

I run on a "fire-hose" approach in both writing and publishing. This idea and practice is to write and publish *prolifically* like the most famous pulp fiction and bestselling authors of all time. You publish everywhere you can as often as you can. And then write and publish some more.

This isn't an approach most people take. And nothing you have to do just because someone else did.

The trick to running an author business (and living itself) is to *find out what works best for you*. Just do that and ignore any reason or opinion from anyone that you should be doing something else. You'll be happier, and in general will be more successful. And after you are a success, then the money rolls in. (Yes, that's not what you're told. But most of the people doing the telling aren't rich, are they?)

You're a success when you've got your first book up. And more successful with all the later books you publish. You're a success when you get your first opt-in to your list. And you're more successful with every additional subscriber, even when people unsubscribe. (But I'll go over how that works a little later.) The point is that you are successfully building your list. With that list you are a little bit more independent from Amazon or anywhere else that wants to control your life from their platform.

So all this book is telling you is what I've found that works *at this time I'm publishing this book*. What I've found out since will only wind up here when I revise this book. What you've found out that works for you, I'll probably never find out – unless you write and publish your own book on this subject.

How to Study This Book

...is in front of your browser with your Instafreebie account opened. Because this is a set of hard-boiled notes. Freshly written at I figure something out. (Made editing a royal pain, BTW.)

When you want to try something (and you should every chance you get) then you can stop reading there and try out what I'm talking about in that section.

That way you can figure out if you can make it work the way I said, or do it better.

This is a hands-on guidebook, not a leisurely modern literature memoir. Think: wrenches and hammers, not ruffled blouses and cute French phrases...

And So...

If four months of participating in other's giveaways and organizing my own giveaways makes anyone an expert, then fine. Otherwise, this is just a collection of observations.

Take them with a grain of salt.

And have fun while you do.

Robert C. Worstell

PS. If you want to keep up with my fire-hose of work, including Instfreebie updates, there's a link in the back to join my list... ;)

The Real Leverage of Book Giveaways

If you've been following Nick Stephenson (or bought his course) you'll know that he got his start by networking with other authors on giveaways and box sets. Networking – remember that. Networking is leverage. *Leverage means more subscribers, more sales, more income from the same written content.*

Instafreebie is a simple way to do this.

Mark Dawson (also one of Stephenson's networked authors) lays out the basics of this:

> "*[A] very effective way of making this work more efficiently is for one of the authors, or an author, to say to maybe nine other authors in their genre.*
>
> *So let's say that I'm doing sci-fi and I say to nine other sci-fi authors that I know, 'I've got an Instafreebie giveaway, would you like to also put a book up. I'll host a page on my website where all of those covers will be available and readers will be able to click on those images and they'll then go through to Instafreebie where they can then download their free book.'*
>
> *The real juice from that is when all of the authors agree that they'll share that page with their list. If I've got 1,000 people on my list, obviously that's a great start but if my other nine collaborators also have 1,000, suddenly I'm 10 timesing my reach to readers who are more likely to like the kinds of books that I'm writing.*"

That's the point of Instafreebie in a nutshell.

You can offer potential subscribers books that they would be interested in and then they opt-in to your list. If they like your books, then they can keep getting emails directly from you.

And since you are in a giveaway with other authors of the same genre, you get more authority as an author regardless of how many years (or months) you've been at this game.

The trick, as I've cover earlier [1]elsewhere[2], is to build a backlist first and then start promoting it. Otherwise, you can start from the get-go with Instafreebie. (I do recommend you thoroughly lay in your habits of writing and reading daily before you start getting in your promotion habit. A logical sequence that works out. I cover the intersection between Draft2Digital[3] and your backlist below. And D2D plus Instafreebie is a match made in heaven for book discovery...)

Where I am at right now is having 36 fiction ebooks published this year under 4 pen names in addition to the 70+ books I've published as author or editor as non-fiction in previous years. The current test is recent fiction against my earlier published non-fiction. And I've spent a few months already working at getting my writing and reading habit ironed in (a bit obvious with those statistics.)

Once I got the decks cleared and the dust settled, I could start promoting on fiction for real. Starting with Instafreebie.

Once I got into Instafreebie, I saw that this isn't just for fiction, but is mostly used for this. And so I can now generate subscribers for my other books as well in the genres of self-improvement, authorship, and business.

What I cover in this text can work for both fiction and non-fiction.

Provided you put it to work and test it for yourself.

Links

- Mark Dawson's January 2017 interview with Ashley Durrer of Instafreebie (podcast with PDF transcript) is available here: https://selfpublishingformula.com/episode-48/

- Katherine Hayton from Alliance of Independent Authors set up a nice review on November 2016 where Instafreebie was giving her much more engaged subscribers to her list, with very few opt-out's. https://selfpublishingadvice.org/book-marketing-with-instafreebie/

---

1. https://livesensical.com/?s=backlist

2. https://livesensical.com/?s=backlist

3. http://livesensical.com/go/draft2digital/

• Elicia Hyder posted on August 2016 about her experiences with Instafreebie. She gives a comparison about how its much cheaper than FB Ads, plus you can start building your own BookBub with a very responsive list. http://www.howtopublishfiction.com/instafreebie-newest-rage-reach-new-readers/

The FAQs for Instafreebie

(See https://support.instafreebie.com[1] – this starts at https://support.instafree-bie.com/category/181-commonly-asked-questions and skips along from there. Hold on, or belt in: this takes off at a sprint...)

Converting Your Book

Instafreebie support suggests using Calibre for conversion. https://support.in-stafreebie.com/article/196-converting-your-file-to-an-epub

The other (better) option is to use Draft2Digital[2], which has much wider support for styles.

Then you can bring it back and clean it up in Calibre[3] (use their Edit Book icon.) It's not necessary though. I've never had a D2D book rejected anywhere due to style or code points.

The four steps I always take to check every single book:

1. Clean up CSS (some rare times, this is a culprit, and D2D leaves a lot of CSS styles in there which aren't necessary. The smaller the file you have, the less likely things to go wrong, plus Amazon won't charge you as much for "shipping."
2. Clean up HTML (fixes anything that doesn't work right, anywhere in the ebook.)
3. Beautify all files (makes it easier to find things and edit them.)
4. Run check for errors (built-in epub check.)

When you send D2D epubs to other aggregators, they all want any link removed except one to your own site. They don't like D2D links, unless you used D2D to send your book to them. (And iTunes doesn't even like you talking about com-

---

1. https://support.instafreebie.com/

2. http://livesensical.com/go/draft2digital/

3. https://calibre-ebook.com/download

petitors, let alone link to them.) This is another good reason to let D2D port your ebook everywhere possible (maybe excepting Amazon.)

Connecting to Your Email Provider

I use Mailerlite as it's cheaper and more robust than MailChimp.

There is a Mailerlite[4] integration guide https://support.instafreebie.com/article/219-mailerlite-faq [5]

This is available on the Plus plan. Otherwise, on the free plan you have to download and manually add your subscribers on your own.

Note that you can set up groups in Mailerlite for each pen name – if you want. At this point I only have a single group for my publishing imprint. I send weekly notice of all the current giveaways, but also have the option of sending an email to anyone who opted in with that pen name, or by book title. Nicely granular.

Instafreebie 101

https://support.instafreebie.com/category/185-instafreebie-101[6]

This is really everything they can think you'll need to get started. This is different than their FAQ pages (https://support.instafreebie.com/category/181-commonly-asked-questions), which are just the common questions.

Author pages

https://support.instafreebie.com/article/172-author-pages[7]

Know that you have an author page for every pen name (on the Pro Plan you can have up to five.) Set up the bio and a link to wherever you can display all your books. This is usually a web page, (like your Blogger blog or other) and can even be Books2Read.com with their new author and book pages.

---

4. http://livesensical.com/go/mailerlite/

5. https://support.instafreebie.com/article/219-mailerlite-faq

6. https://support.instafreebie.com/category/185-instafreebie-101

7. https://support.instafreebie.com/article/172-author-pages

Customize Your Claim Pages

https://support.instafreebie.com/article/16-customizing-your-claim-pages[8]

This is a nice way to let your readers know you care about them. There's not a lot to do here, but it wraps up your pages nicely. Note that you only can have a single claim page for all your pen names. I put my publishing imprint here, so that they are all under one roof.

Instafreebie Starter Kit

https://support.instafreebie.com/article/104-instafreebie-starter-kit[9]

Once you get all the basics in, then these steps are highly recommended.

Essentially, this walks you through getting a book uploaded and then making it available as an offer. To join group giveaways, you have to have the book uploaded to Instafreebie, but you don't have to have it available for everyone. The pages on Giveaways (https://support.instafreebie.com/article/179-giveaway-101) tells you al about the types of giveaways – outreach, private, and custom. Study this before you join other giveaways.

Joining Group Giveaways

Essentially, this is a must. As many as possible, as a general rule. The point is Heinlein's last rule, which is to always keep your story on sale – this means discoverability. And Instafreebie is a key way to keep all your books discoverable. Because you at least want free books out there so they find your other ones. Follow through the steps of getting your books into all possible giveaways.

See the points below on Draft2Digital and their unlimited book referrals through every book you publish with them. Use their ebook versions to upload to Instafreebie to ensure your backmatter allows them to find your books. Also, you book should always have a direct opt-in so people can simply and directly join your mailing list.

---

8. https://support.instafreebie.com/article/16-customizing-your-claim-pages

9. https://support.instafreebie.com/article/104-instafreebie-starter-kit

Rolling Your Own Group Giveaway

https://support.instafreebie.com/article/215-how-to-organize-an-instafreebie-group-giveaway[10]

Once you get the hang of submitting your various ebooks to the various giveaways, then the next step is to get your own giveaway going. This will tell you a lot about marketing your book and is a key way to network with other authors.

The whole point of Giveaways is to build subscriber lists. And this is where you make your monthly investment in Instafreebie pay off. The point is to dive in and start joining giveaways and also to create group giveaways of your own.

Verified Organizer Giveaways.

https://support.instafreebie.com/article/220-verified-organizer-faq[11]

Read this and click the link at the bottom to fill our their form. This status is only approved on an individual basis. Essentially, this is for someone who is well-established and contributing to the Instafreebie network, with lots of books there and lots of giveaways created.

The essential benefits are to give greater control over email lists. Here's their description:

> *"Group Giveaways that are run by a Verified Organizer may have special requirements for participating authors. These Group Giveaways allow the Verified Organizer to decide whether or not readers will be given the opportunity to opt in to the mailing lists of Author Team members. According to the settings on the Group Giveaway, all giveaways created for the Group Giveaway will be either optional or no opt-in. Verified Organizers can also choose whether or not readers will be given the option to subscribe to the organizer's mailing list"*

---

10. https://support.instafreebie.com/article/215-how-to-organize-an-instafreebie-group-giveaway

11. https://support.instafreebie.com/article/220-verified-organizer-faq

Meaning that to earn that verified title, you can massively increase your subscriptions by getting everyone's opt-in's,or at least give the readers that option.

Refer and Earn Program

https://support.instafreebie.com/article/92-refer-and-earn-program[12]

When you go all-in on this program, as I have, this is a key point to lower your monthly costs. By getting people to sign up for Instafreebie, you drop your own costs for a little bit, for a little while. So this is ongoing promotion on your part.

Since Instafreebie has been number-crunched to be the most efficient way of getting new subscribers (costing less than Facebook Ads), then they become a regular weekly/monthly work on your part to build your own subscriber list.

The general plan would be to have your books as part of all possible giveaways (one per pen-name, at least) every single month of the year. And also run regular giveaways of your own during that time as well.

Having No List is No Problem

Sure, you are expected to promote to all your list to get subscribers for everyone. And since no one can tell what you email to others (without being on your list) then this is basically an honor-based platform. Obviously, if you could you would. The more you pay to Instafreebie, the more they want to help you by promoting your giveaways. Every week, they send out a newsletter telling about the giveaways. And they promote through their app as well (which of course, you should recommend...)

The Added Cost of Multiple Pen Names

My recommended approach is to have multiple pen names with a backlist for each. So each pen name should have an "outreach" giveaway that shows up on the author page and is perennially available. (Yes, you can change this out at any time.) In addition to that, you put up a couple or few more that you can use to put into various giveaways.

---

12. https://support.instafreebie.com/article/92-refer-and-earn-program

This brings you into the upper range of what Instafreebie supports. Their Pro version is 50 bucks a month to get 5 pen names. One is your own, obviously. Great for all your non-fiction. And I'd suggest three pen names where you can take three genres to master them, using your stories by each pen name to concentrate on on one each. You could take the physical plot structures[13] (Romance, Mystery-Detective, Adventure) to master these forms. Or just work up a set of stories for a particular genre you like to read and then concentrate on getting these stories as good as you can.

The reason for pen-names is also to excuse your earliest work. Your later work will always be better, as you are constantly working to improve every story better than the last. So if a particular pen name has gotten no sales, you could simply start over.

But You Only Get Five At a Time

Probably because no one knows that this is the way to success. Unfortunately, the truly prolific authors will use dozens and dozens of different pen names during their career. Particularly in genre fiction, where the emphasis is on particular audience expectations rather than a writing style. Boilerplate romance novels are like this.

Instafreebie is useful, because you can change out your pen names if one isn't working for you. You even have a one-time option to get a permanent url for a given pen name. But I'd suggest (obviously) that you don't. Because it's permanent, and won't change after that. Once you have a brand, great. Until then, you can change out your pen name specifics all you want.

Right now, I have all five taken, although one is just starting out. Non-fiction, Humor (Satire/Parody), Fantasy, Science Fiction, Mystery-Detective. And that prompts me to get back into writing daily, every day. Then using the rest of my time to get publishing and promotion done (other than my nightly reading and watching TV series.)

---

13. https://livesensical.com/plots-personal-inspiration-popular-fiction-writing/

But with that amount of investment going out every month, I'm prompted to get a lot more out of Instafreebie when I do.

Note

Instafreebie isn't for Kindle Select/Unlimited Books, except their free days – and Instafreebie giveaways can't be shorter than three days. Having Kindle-centric books reportedly means you can't even sell the book through your own site (unless your sales page only has that Kindle link on it – but even then...) You can only give away books during your "free days" and so you can realistically just set the time for that giveaway for those five days every 90. And it's probably not worth it. Better would be to giveaway another book that isn't in Select. (Or just skip Select altogether.)

Instafreebie For Audience and List Building

Instafreebie is one of the most overlooked audience and list-builders for authors. Those who know about it and use is are building their subscriber base by using one of the fastest and least expensive ways known.

First, Why Do You Need a Mailing List?

Because Amazon, Facebook, Twitter, and the rest are changing all the time. You can't rely on them to allow you to contact your buyers or followers. Most, in fact, don't want you to. Unless its through them. They all have restrictions against directly asking people for contact data.

Ask yourself this: What would you do if Amazon quit tomorrow? Is that your only income source for book sales? Could you contact your buyers to tell them about your next book coming out?

Facebook could shut down, and so could Twitter, and any or all of the other social media platforms.

Would you be screwed, or would you be prepared?

As you build your own subscriber list, you can cushion that blow when it (inevitably) happens.

The real side benefit is that by mailing to your own list, you don't have to advertise to get people to buy your books (well, not as much.) Because you already have a fan base that you've built up who have bought your books and want more of them. You have built your own Book Bub, actually. Why pay for their services when you can simply send out an email that costs you only time?

If you have a subscriber list, you have a business. If you don't, you are living on borrowed time.

Free, Plus, and Pro Plans to Get Subscribers

There are three plans:

Basic – Free. Where you can get your books up and join in on giveaways, but not integrate your mailing list.

- *Unlimited giveaways and distribution at no additional cost*

- *Instafreebie acceleration to the right readers*

- *Customer support for readers*

- *1 pen name and author page*

Plus – For $20 per month, you get a single author pen-name and can integrate either MailerLite or MailChimp, so that your subscribers are immediately sent to your list and so you can set them up with a response. Contrast this with the free plan where you'd have to export from Instafreebie and then import into your mailing list.

- *Everything in Basic +*

- *Add subscribers to a mailing list*

- *Optional MailerLite or MailChimp integration*

- *Fully customizable giveaways*

- *Track giveaway success*

Pro – For $50 per month, you get five author pen-names with author pages. Un-stated here is that they pay more attention to your giveaways and you in general (or I'm led to believe that, anyway.)

- *Everything in Plus +*

- *Personalized giveaway branding*

- *Up to 5 pen names and author pages*

Author Pages and Pen Names

On these author pages, they list the books you've made available for those pen names and make them available for anyone to claim and potentially sign up to your mailing list.

One of the great things you can do with the author page at Instafreebie is plug it into the "follow this author" link at books2read.com (created and run by the brilliant people at Draft2Digital.com) Someone interested in following you can claim a book to get on your mailing list – or just get a book to see if they like your style. It's up to you to also include opt-in links inside the book itself.

Your Instafreebie author page can be edited. One thing to suggest here is to not nail down a specific address for that pen name. Because 1) most authors who use pen names acquire far more than five, and 2) you'll change pen names if you aren't getting a result, because the reason for pen names is to get started at all, regardless of your skill. And so you don't put your own name on all your writing until later when you are very, very good at writing. However, authors like O. Henry, and Louis L'Amour were famous and known by their pen name instead of their real one for almost their entire writing career.

Books2Read.com gives you author pages and book pages for each book. And they are interlinked, so that author and book pages refer to each other. Obviously, having your Books2Read pages link to your Instafreebie pages should give you a lot of SEO link love and more subscribers.

Promotional Use of Instafreebie with Draft2Digital Links

A next point comes up is to keep your Instafreebie offers updated with your books on Draft2Digital. With each book through Draft2Digital[1], you have the option of having "Also by [pen name/author]" page at the back of every book. Later books are automatically added to your ebook.

This makes each of your books have a sales-linked page of related titles.

---

1. http://livesensical.com/go/draft2digital/

All your giveaways, if run through Draft2Digital, are linked in promotions to the rest of your books. Meaning you are now enabling your backlist sales without having to send them to Amazon for your other works. (Note that the book pages Draft2Digital creates for you automatically also list the other books – linked to their B2R sales pages – for each book. Meaning you only have recommendations for your own books there.

Conversely, your author page on Instafreebie can also cross-link back to your Books2Read author page, where they can also find all the other books. And buy them. Which takes a lot of the problem of creating sales pages on your own blog for those books.

Here's examples:

- Instafreebie author page: https://www.instafreebie.com/discover/author/23300/c_c_brower

- Books2Read author page: https://books2read.com/ap/xqOrdn/C-C-Brower

If you're using redirect links, it would be sensible to send potential subscribers to your Instafreebie page, and subscribers to the books2read page. If this ever changes, then you just change the address on the redirect link.

Best Practices – Mostly Common Sense and Manners

I did contact support as I couldn't find any "best practices" write ups or even how-to's on working with Group Giveaways. I suspect because the platform is so new, and so underutilized.

Support at Instafreebie is recognized as being friendly, even enthusiastic. And that is exactly what I found. I sent them a long email and got a long one in return. Here's key data I got:

- *Giveaways can run for any time period* (some as short as the Amazon 3 days), but the average time is about a month. (I mentioned that I saw one graph where the giveaways trended down over that month on a per day basis. I'll verify this when my own first giveaway starts running.)

• *It's a best practice to send out only a regular weekly email* to announce these to your own list. And obviously, that won't be the only thing on them. The main idea is to enable them to find more books to read (especially for free) and where to find your backlist of other books. I discussed the recommended Twitter practice of sending out several times per day, but Twitter is coming down on that practice, saying they want original tweets each time.

• *Along with the email, you should Tweet/Plus/etc. the current group giveaways you are part of every week.* The main point of this is to pay it forward to promote Instafreebie, but also allow others to retweet/ share your social postings through their own social networks. Social media isn't known for getting book sales, unless people are very interactive with a select group of followers there. (For me, I'd rather be writing.)

• *Instafreebie will feature recommended giveaways.* This is done on the home page. And so it's suggested that you start on a Sunday and end on a Tuesday. Because the features run Monday to Monday. They also send out a Friday newsletter with the active giveaways, but that isn't so date-sensitive.

Instafreebie also has guidelines for selecting featured giveaways:

• At least 10 unique Authors participating

• Authors should have their own accounts to protect their content and protect readers

• Group Giveaway is free for authors to join

• Final image graphic to share must be book/genre/author focused, and 1500px by 500px (length by height)

• Final duration dates of promotion should be displayed on the graphic/page

• In accordance with our Community Guidelines[2], final image graphic may not include graphic nudity (the Instafreebie staff reserves the right to reject any image graphic at our discretion)

• Instafreebie Group Giveaway must be live for a minimum of 3 days after the date of the feature

• Instafreebie Group Giveaway Details Page link (link should begin with "instafreebie.com/[3]") and graphic must be sent a week minimum before your feature date

The common sense and manners comes in from what I've found so far:

• *Leave a comment when you enter your book and when you approve others books.* This keeps it real. There is little more frustrating when a person is an anonymous boob as giveaway administrator.

• *I like weekly updates from the admin about how the giveaway is going.* How many and so on. There is an internal comment box where you can send him data, and auto-send this (if you want) to the rest of the authors in the giveaway as well.

• *Submit books that are only what is wanted.* And be respectful of the boobs who don't when you reject them. Clarify your requirements if you have to. Don't submit a bodice-ripping romance to a Young Adult Fantasy giveaway. Make sure your book genre is appropriate.

How Many and How Often You Should Giveaway

As often as you can, like all the time. Seriously.

---

2. https://instafreebie.com/about/communityguidelines

3. http://instafreebie.com/groupgiveaway/view

This is the advantage to having lots of books to choose from for each pen name. Try at least two if not four books for each author (remember, this advice is for short stories, but you could create previews out of novels as well.) That said, I also have seen people giving away boxed sets.

In general, the same authors don't show up for every giveaway. And if some do, their lists are changing every week. Plus and minus. So you are better off being on as many giveaways as you can all the time as a participant. Just set up a system (like your weekly newsletter) where you can link to that week's giveaways and tell them about it. I keep a page on my site that I'll update every week that links to current giveaways.

The main point: *you can't get on too many of these.* There are too many authors, each with different lists. And those lists aren't static. Also, you are putting up several books by different pen names in different genres. Choices. If they don't opt-in (and it's suggested you give them a choice) then they have the promotion to your other books by that author/pen-name in every book.

As far as organizing giveaways, my current strategy is to have them running every month, about 10 per year. Right now, I have 5 in the works, and plan to set up some early giveaways as soon as I can, since the major booksellers do seasonal approaches, leaving off in January and August. That makes these prime time for Indie authors to push their books on to the big bestseller lists. And the best way to do this is to build a huge and devoted fan base that you can reach through email.

Otherwise, there is Halloween themed (horror genre) giveaways for October and Holiday/Christmas themed giveaway for November/December.

The other approach is to build giveaways for the genres which are under-represented. (Like anything non-romance.) Business and Non-fiction often have nothing running. But a lot of authors have some of these books around. I had over 30 authors sign up for my "How To..." giveaway in 24 hours. A few tests will show you supply and demand for these. Then I'll know the "sweet spots".

Again: keep your books in "discovery mode" at all times by joining all possible giveaways that are appropriate. And meanwhile organize and run at least one giveaway at all times. These won't take but minutes per week to maintain, but should result in hundreds of opt-in's weekly when they get going.

Should You Organize Private Group Giveaways?

Short answer: maybe.

You will only gain the readers from the other authors. If you make it private and invite people you've worked with before, you may have essentially the same list and so might not get all that many new subscribers, as their readers have already seen your content before.

Also, private giveaways aren't featured by Instafreebie. So you aren't going to get that bump in claims – which is often more than any single author can create in a giveaway.

So the point of having a list of other Instafreebie author names to invite authors is to more likely ensure that your giveaway has your minimum of 10 authors who have their own account – so Instafreebie may feature your giveaway.

I only bring this up as something I've noted from editing this book. This isn't a guide to networking beyond Instafreebie, although some of the ideas here well help you get started in that direction.

(Stay tuned for updates by joining my list with the links at the back of this book...)

Instafreebie Errata - Tips, Tricks, Strategies

These notes started from getting active on Instafreebie (and getting over 130 opt-ins in less than two weeks, starting with knowing nothing about this stuff. I'm now over a thousand in these few months and regularly adding subscribers daily. (Cost? About $120, around 10 cents each.)

The original idea of this article was to keep track of what I was doing so I could improve on what worked. Also, to help others from the knowledge I've gained. Obviously, it's grown into a book.

This list is roughly in order of how I discovered things, and got answers from Instafreebie support to my many questions.

You'll see as you go down this list that I repeat some datums more than once, and some that are already in this book. Repetition is a good method of learning, and may give additional insight or compound the data from before.

How to Study This Section

I realized as I was editing this for the umpteenth time that my prose is pretty rugged at times. Here's how to get the most out of this chapter:

1. Take a section that is something you'd like to test for yourself.
2. Figure out the action steps and take them. See what results you get, how workable that description is.
3. Then come back and re-write that section in your own words.

It will all make a lot more sense that way.

And, again, email me if it still doesn't – or you'd like to send me your revision. (Join my list at the end of this book...)

The Tips

- **Read and follow directions.** Every. Single. Time. Fill out everything the way you want to represent yourself or your books. This is a well thought-out service.

The directions are simple. Make sure you understand them and don't assume anything. Best is to first go through the FAQs at support.instafreebie.com[1]

- **Be respectful and communicative.** Add comments to everything. *Treat people as you'd like to be treated.* Organizers like to be thanked. Submitters like to be thanked. Leave comments when you do something, even if it's only leaving a tweet. That tells the organizer you are working at this. Otherwise, (s)he's going to figure that you didn't even try. You want the organizer to even invite you to one of their later giveaways. *People like nice, they hate trolls.* "You catch more flies with honey than vinegar."

- **Provide at least one giveaway book for each of the genres you are writing in.** At least one per pen-name. Recall that Blockbusters and Bestsellers are pan-genre - they have some of everything in them. The general strategy is to write in one pen name for each of the three physical plot structures (Mystery, Romance, Adventure.)[2] And you write in short stories and put these up (even if they are collections of flash fiction in order to fit the KDP 2500 word minimum.) Just note that they are short stories in the description. *Be painfully honest and transparent at everything you do.* You'll get more respect and build more trust that way.

- **Don't worry about genre's you don't write in.** I do write in Contemporary, but don't write in YA. Stick to your strengths. I do have one cozy Romance (no obvious sex in it) but the rest of my books have romance as a sub-plot. Many of the YA giveaways are very specific about this, as YA doesn't have graphic sex in them, and the protagonist is a teenager or young adult (under 30.) Also, don't write just one book in a genre and expect your potential readers to be satisfied. I could easily write erotica, but haven't. I'm mastering the Romance genre before I get anywhere near erotica. But I'm getting my Fantasy, Science Fiction, and Detective chops before that. Until I have at least three books in any particular genre, I wouldn't worry about publishing any. (And by "book" I mean a story long enough to publish on Amazon – about 2500 words.) When you do, readers will then look up the others in that series. (*Always write in series and serials.*) That is the point of series and serials - to push sales of your other works.

---

1. http://support.instafreebie.com/

2. https://livesensical.com/plots-personal-inspiration-popular-fiction-writing/

- **Your best approach as an author with no lists is to organize and run your own group giveaways.** While you're at it, run several. Set them up months ahead, and in times where no one else is running a giveaway for your genre. There are a lot more authors than there are giveaway organizers. And most organizers only run one giveaway at a time. The "top dogs" seem to run about four (spaced out over months, not all at once.) Look over the giveaways for the genres you've written in (you have three genres you can assign per book) and see what any organizers are providing.

- **Join as many giveaways as you can.** As above, I started at 1 person on my list and then got over 130 opt-ins in less than two weeks once I joined Instafreebie giveaways. (At this writing, four months in, I'm over 1200.) You just send out to whatever your list is, plus Twitter and FB and Google+ and anywhere else you can, even if you don't have much of a following. *And then leave a comment in the giveaway that you did something.* There's really no stigma about starting with nothing. As you build what you have, then you'll get a lot more something to work with. This last week, I send out a message to my 130+ people and got 90+ to go to my web-page with all the Instafreebie giveaways on it. And some of those readers went to Amazon, iTunes, and Kobo. That felt good, as you can imagine.

- **Track your giveaways links with Bit.ly** Set up a bit.ly account (free) and create a bit.ly link for each giveaway you are part of. When you add a "+" (plus sign) after the bit.ly link, you will be able to find how many times that link was accessed and when. Organizers have this data on their dashboard. Your bit.ly short link will redirect your viewers and track them for you.

- **Read the requirements for the giveways you're joining - carefully.** I earlier set up a giveaway for Christmas or Holiday *themed* books. The two genres were contemporary and fantasy. And constantly had people submitting everything other than a themed book. One author submitted nearly a dozen Romance novels to it, which had nothing even about winter in them. (Duh?) Now I know who that is, and her spammy practices. (Why she is giving away that many books all at once is another questionable practice.)

- Set your books up with Draft2Digital[3]. Here you can auto-update links to your other books. They use Books2Read[4] links, which then tell you how many times they are accessed. And Books2Read also creates book pages and authors pages. Your Book2Read author page can be your website page for Instafreebie, and your Instafreebie pen name can go onto your Books2Read author pages. So readers looking up your author will be sent either to your other books by that pen-name, or to free books so they can opt-in. This is exactly what happens. People look up your other books when they get a free one. And if you're sending them via a Books2Read link, you'll know where they went to check out that book - and preferably buy it. (If you're exclusive, just use Draft2Digital to only publish to KDP. Again, might seem counter-intuitive, but when you have a dozen books up there and cranking out one every week or so, it can be a real pain to have to update all of the earlier ones every time with live links where they can be bought.)

- Use a Publishing Imprint instead of an author name or pen name. If you don't want to opt for the $50/mo. Instafreebie level, then consider doing the $20 level and setting your one author name as your publishing imprint. Then put your author/pen-name in the title of the book. For me, it's "Midwest Journal Press" and the book would be "Make Yourself Great Again by Dr. Robert C. Worstell" - see? I found a group of authors who runs under a single brand name and has about 8 different authors, who are all busy writing. One (great) book collection they offered was from an author who I already knew from her blog and found I loved her books. Of course, you are then (sorely) tempted to buy as she has maybe another couple-dozen books in this and other series. And that was the whole point. Those authors are probably paying someone monthly to get their books into Instafreebie giveaways and also send out their emails promoting their books.

- But stick to your guns in organizing a genre-specific giveaway. Deny books that are too off-beat. One thing you don't need is people being run away from your giveaway by erotica, LGBT, or explicit material – or vice versa. Readers know what genres they like and that is why genres developed – to meet reader expectations.

---

3. http://livesensical.com/go/draft2digital/

4. http://books2read.com/

Romance covers are all mostly the same – one or two or more half-undressed people (usually male chests and six-packs.) Someone looking for SF or sword-and-sorcerer fantasy will go away if all they see is romantic covers, even if they are "romantic" fantasy (light on fantasy, heavy on romance.)

This is the point of being professional and paying attention to details. *Always work toward the best possible reader experience.*

- **How to leave blurbs.** When you submit a book, it's suggested you give a blurb. "Great cover, nice description" isn't a useful blurb. It won't help people get that book. You're going to have to download their book and read it as least as much as an editor, so you can write a blurb that will help readers get that book. The trick is that you have to download the book in order to read it so you can have an opinion. So you should actually claim the books already approved, read it, write a blurb. You can only leave a blurb (one per author) inside the admin page for the giveaway itself. You do this on an upcoming or current or completed giveaway. Then there is a nice page so you can see the one's you got and the one's you gave. Here is where you pay your karma forward. This is one of the hidden points to Instafreebie. *You have to give in order to get.*

- **The core point of Instafreebie is** *networking***.** It's not list-building. That's just a side benefit. Same for increasing sales. Sure, the money is nice. The point is to build a collaborative network of fellow authors. This is a cumulative effect is exponential, not additive. Meaning that it increases well beyond just the lists numbers of the authors you add. The math goes like this: every person is able to effectively work with somewhere between 100 to 250 people (called Dunbar's number[5].)

When you add authors who are knowingly building their own network, then you increase your own by a *factor*, not just by a single person. Your work then becomes more than the joy you personally get from writing. Or the freedom of nearly unlimited passive income supporting your gifts. The point of your work is to fill and train your network so they fill and train theirs - and so on to potentially infinity. And as these networks grow, they then build by factors into a scope that is probably impossible to imagine. Yes, that last point even surprises me.

---

5. https://en.wikipedia.org/wiki/Dunbar%27s_number

- **Making your free book exclusive to Instafreebie is a good thing.** On the books I've put up there, they are full price elsewhere, but can be gotten for free only through Instafreebie. And so they are marked "Exclusive" with a free red banner on top of the book cover image. So your book stands out on any giveaway. Simple, yes? The only two books I have that are free everywhere (out of more than a dozen) aren't exclusive. My books show up as exclusive in every giveaway they are entered in. Nice. *Note*: you do have to manually turn this feature on for every giveaway you join.

- **Updated Emails per EU laws is another good thing.** This recent General Data Protection Regulation (GDPR) has made Instafreebie require that you not automatically make people give you their emails. You still can, but your giveaway won't be featured on the site. Before this, Instafreebie had a note that enforcing opt-ins would result in higher complaints and unsubscribes. Frankly, I don't see why anyone would make it mandatory opt-in, anyway. (Probably a hangover from old conventional wisdom when it wasn't an option.) Last time I checked, I was getting nearly 40% opt-in from all these claimed downloads. And again, with books2read links updated by Draft2Digital, these ebooks are all linked into all other related books and so are promotion pieces by themselves. And they also have opt-in links in there. This is simple good promotion.

- **Giving Blurbs is limited.** 1) You can't blurb your own books. 2) You can only blurb another author-account once - meaning that if you have several books by the same "author", you can only blurb one of them. 3) You can only (apparently) blurb an author who is in the same giveaway as you are. "Author" is any pen-name. So someone who is going the less expensive route of having a single publisher imprint that covers several authors, only one of those actual authors can get a blurb from another Instafreebie account. The Pro version has 5 pen names and so has 5 chances to get blurbs from a single other account. This is one area which could definitely be improved, since blurbs show up on the giveaway pages. Again, don't leave "Nice cover. Great description." as a blurb, as you're wasting a great networking opportunity. Leave something you would like to receive.

- **Getting Your Subscribers Auto-Enrolled Is Simple.** But I had to ask support to find it. It is possible only with the paid plans. But even then it doesn't work every time. Every single book can go to its own mailing list if you want. Setting a default mailing list for all your books is a good backup. Otherwise, your mailing list can be set individually when you enter a book. (Of course, without a default, those subscribers just sit there and still have to be manually imported) And this is good for having multiple pen names under the Pro plan. (You're going to have to manually import your subscribers under the free plan.) Again, you can set a default list for everything, which works if you don't specify anything for that particular book. On your dashboard page, click on your name and click the *Settings* link. Then click on *Mail Service Integrations* to find it.

- **Getting Granular Email Data on Subscribers**. You can get what book and what giveaway people join your list for. It's all there in Instafreebie for a manual download. But I asked how to make it automatic and got this reply:

> *To have this information appear when subscribers are automatically sent to Mailerlite, you'll have to add columns for this information in your subscriber list on Mailerlite. You'll have to add the following fields, and then you should see that information filled when they are sent to MailerLite. Add columns for 'Book Title' and 'Giveaway.' The merge tags in Mailer-Lite will look like $book_title, and $giveaway. If you want he can also add Genre (merge tag $genre), and Source (merge tag $source). Genre is book genre, and source will always be Instafreebie.*

The obvious benefit is to send special emails to those people who liked that pen name, or if that pen name co-authors with another one. After awhile, you can also see which books do best for you and which type of giveaways do best, etc. Tailoring emails to those type of subscribers is what email is all about - building relationships.

- **Running A/B Tests on Giveaway Descriptions.** Maybe you could improve your description and get more downloads. An A/B test seems a smart move to compare which description converts best. Half get one and half get the other. Currently, only the giveaway organizer can run these, and on any book there in addition to his own. Maybe you want to offer this as a service for people during your giveaway. At least run it on your own.

- Getting Instafreebie to Recommend Your Giveaway. Don't know how I over-looked this, until I came back to this page as my own go-to reference and found it missing. Here's part of an email I got from the wonderful people at Instafreebie Support:

> *We have our own personal guidelines when it comes to group giveaways which helps us select our featured ones:*
>
> • *At least 10 unique Authors participating*
>
> • *Authors should have their own accounts to protect their content and protect readers*
>
> • *Group Giveaway is free for authors to join*
>
> • *Final image graphic to share must be book/genre/author focused, and 1500px by 500px (length by height)*
>
> • *Final duration dates of promotion should be displayed on the graphic/ page*
>
> • *In accordance with our Community Guidelines[6], final image graphic may not include graphic nudity (the Instafreebie staff reserves the right to reject any image graphic at our discretion)*
>
> • *Instafreebie Group Giveaway must be live for a minimum of 3 days after the date of the feature*
>
> • *Instafreebie Group Giveaway Details Page link (link should begin with "instafreebie.com/[7]") and graphic must be sent a week minimum before your feature date*

and...

---

6. *https://instafreebie.com/about/communityguidelines*

7. *http://instafreebie.com/groupgiveaway/view*

In terms of the start day of a group giveaway, we haven't looked too much into this. But, a common trend among organizers is to start giveaways on the first day of the month or on a Sunday. If you want to be featured by Instafreebie, I would generally recommend starting on a Sunday and ending on a Tuesday. This is because we feature group giveaways on our homepage from Monday until the Monday of the next week regardless of the day it is featured in our newsletter.

As I review this, this really points to having giveaways at least two weeks long (or 17 days.) This gives Instafreebie two chances to feature your giveaway. I'm running a set of 10 day "blitzes" right now and that will give me more data. Elsewhere, support has told me the average giveaway runs for a month. So theoretically, you can run 12 giveaways a year with just slight overlaps.

- **Leeches in Giveaways.** That's someone who is only there for the ride, to get claims without doing anything. Only the organizer can see these. The current giveaway I'm running has just under 30% actually promoting. Adding in those who promote but get no claims (not technically leeching) you wind up just over 21% (And one such leech was a group of professional authors who have banded together to promote their books. Whoever is doing their promotion is faking it.) The way around this is to collect the email addresses of your participating authors. Some do this with an Google form on the description.

Since these percentages are running close to the Pareto Principle, you can't just get some resentment going and back up into just being a control freak and limiting who can join to "only those with big lists." Again, everyone has to start somehow. And the more books you have in the giveaway, the more people are likely to click on something.

- **Leechers as Organizers.** I've mentioned the organizer "control freaks" above. Add to this the people who insist you pay them for the opportunity to join their giveaway (money or your email address.) Truly, truly dumb. They are leeching off the Instafreebie platform. Because if you don't see a giveaway you'd like to join, the solution is always to start your own giveaway and run it the way you want it. See the points about limits above. Same for people who use Instafreebie to then collect submissions they run on a different platform. Of course, they don't get recommended by Instafreebie and miss out. Kinda like taking your playmates and toys to go to your own small and exclusive sandbox. You just miss out on potential friends and networking opportunities. And I simply avoid those "limited" organizers. Not worth my time.

The main point is to keep these as open as possible and realize that 20% are going to give you 80% of your claims. People who try to suck the life out of the giveaway, or those who don't contribute, all have their own problems. Work out how to reward the productive individuals and form a team with them. You have to give before you can get - and always give open-handedly (not expecting anything in return.) The object is to really enjoy your business activities as much as you enjoy writing and publishing. Stay away from leechers as you can, but also live and let live.

- **How To Get Yourself Blacklisted**. Leechers are those who blatantly or quietly don't contribute to the mutual-trust environment of Instafreebie. Sure, you don't have to join the giveaways that are run by control freaks, or are out to monetize the Instafreebie platform for themselves. But when organizing your giveaways, you can quickly compile lists of people who aren't doing anything to promote, but have a lot of books there. The worst offender on my current giveaway has 7 books there and has done diddly-squat promotion. Meanwhile, they pulled down nearly 10 percent of the total claims.

Does this mean that others would get more claims if they weren't there? Maybe. Pointing it out to them broadly is one way to put attention on it. Now I see why people want a simple form filled out so they can contact authors directly off-line. It would make the administration smoother, since there is no DM to use on this site, and you can't get emails from them.

When I get a few of these under my belt, I'll have a short list of repeat offenders to watch for, and even block. These will be by name, giveaway, date, etc. That particular account that has 7 books up there might get some action. When they are taking 10% of the total, and are the top claimed books, then would this "cut off my nose to spite my face"?

Regardless, I'll have my list...

- **When a Group Giveaway Falls Flat**... I found myself surprised by a giveaway that had a short lead time and only myself and one other author actually put any books into it. (I was under several pen-names.) So I made lemonade of out it. The solution was to do extra promotion for it, syndicating it out to social media via Buffer on a daily basis and changing the description to say that I would be adding more books every single day, while pointing up the idea that the giveaway was only running for 10 days. I'm also changing the graphic every day with a count-down. The test has a bit to run, but it should do fine. I also told my list to give me any requests for any book I had published and I'd put it in the giveaway. So that helped out.

And I found out that sending just to people who were routinely clicking through my email links (something that was difficult to find out on my earlier email provider) gave me a very good response. Also, asking other authors in a separate non-fiction giveaway scheduled a month later got me another author to join. We'll see...

- **Aggregating Author Names with a Google Form.** I've talked about this earlier. All I'd seen were organizers enforcing getting email addresses from people in order to join their giveaway - along with data like size of list and book data. That always irritated me, as it was punishing people for being starting authors with no list. But checking with Support (who are always very wonderful native English speakers) confirmed that they couldn't give out email addresses and I was on my own to contact them. Other than opting into their list via claiming their book. I then tried out Google Forms, found them simple to set up (and even setting an option for being alerted when someone filled it out.) So I put this as a free optional form in the description of all my upcoming giveaways. I'll keep adding to this list and eventually have one that is all authors that I can contact about joining giveaways. (Separately from that, I have a list someone had sent out to their project people, who'd also given their address. Because they sent it from their gmail account with all the people added as CC's instead of BCC's or blind carbon copy. Probably do a trial mailing to these to see if they are interested.)

The point is that if you treat people nicely, then you'll get a nice response. Force them to do something and the effect is "they'll run away just as long as you are chasing."

Put this link at the top of your giveaways as a non-required option. And then put it in your comments of every giveaway on the last day, both the one's you're running and the ones you're part of. The people who raise their hands are the ones you want. They are the most active ones, and the ones who probably have good lists or at least active in building them. What you won't get are the leechers, the get-rich-quick crowd. That's real networking.

Right now, I've getting more opt-in's by giving that link on the last day of a giveaway – that figures, since it's a live link in the comments, and isn't in the description as just text.

- **Analyzing Your Subscribers for Best Books.** This is a bit tricky, but more straightforward than you might think. By taking your total Instafreebie subscriber list, you can see which books and which giveaways gave you the best result. Of course, you may have several books on offer in any giveaway, but the ones you see were the first where they opted in to your list. But that will get you started.

The variables are that some giveaways are promoted better by the authors and Instafreebie than others. The reasons are various. Comparing those giveaways with each other will tell you a lot. (See below for that analysis.)

By downloading your complete list and opening it up in a spreadsheet, you can start by finding which of your books and which giveaways were the best. Then make sure that you are part of any giveaway like this. If no one is offering one, then start these up yourself. You should have your books in all possible giveaways at all times. Better than this is to have your best-claimed books in the best possible giveaways by genre. Cross comparing your completed giveaways with your subscribers will start giving you broad hints about where to test next.

Note: Those blank lines in the spreadsheet where a giveaway should be? You need to go in and set a name for your first giveaway. A blank line means there is no name present.

- **Preliminary Results of Giveaway Analyses:** Average length right now from data to hand tends to be about 25 days on giveaways. This summer has a lot of two-week giveaways. But a small handful of two-month giveaways are pulling the length back. In general, get your books everywhere they belong, the more the better. Then make sure you actually contribute to all the giveaways you join. I have a blog page of all the giveaways I'm part of, each with Bitly-shortened links so I can see which are getting clicks. This has them compete on their banners and genres, like book covers.

Having a long lead time for giveaways seems to get more books entered. Right now, it seems that putting them out about three months in advance seems a useful investment. How much you want to deal with giveaways will determine how much you want to invest in these. The general rule is to always have one of your own giveaways running, and joining in all the giveaways you can. Meanwhile, collect emails from authors to invite them to yours.

- **Verified Organizers and Giving Value.** It's not hard to create giveaways. Running them should be a regular give and take between you and your authors. Again, it goes back to treating people as you'd like to be treated. Becoming a verified organizer is a great label to have. Like "exclusive" on your book, it gives authors another reason to opt-in to your giveaway. One thing Instafreebie looks for is interaction between the organizer and the authors. And giving value is another way to help your authors learn through this process and build up their own list. As well, they will trust you to give you their email address. If that weren't enough, you have the option of enabling the readers to join your list as well as the authors!

One suggestion would be to take each of these hints above and suggest them in the comments box every few days to help your authors out.

- **Related Email List Tips.** While Instafreebie is great for getting giveaway lovers, our trick is to do careful gardening of our crop to weed out those that aren't wanted. Because once you pass the limit on your free list, you're paying to send out emails to these people. That's whether they open anything or not. It may seem counterintuitive to be removing people from your list weekly (kinda like spending months writing a novel only to give it away.) What you don't want is people who sign up and never open anything. Or later, they quit opening your stuff. Now I can see where people get busy, so this is what I've set up on Mailerlite that I work with weekly:

- I set up a segment that has a) anyone who has gotten 5 or more emails from me and never opened anything, and b) anyone who hasn't opened up an email in the last 90 days. That segment auto-updates regularly, so I have an accurate recount every few hours.

- I send out a short email entitled "Still Interested?" and a short explanation that will show up in their email header that starts: "...I noticed you haven't opened anything we've sent you recently..." There is an unsubscribe link on the line immediately after that (which is there to avoid jerks complaining that I'm sending spam.) And then I tell them how I understand completely if they don't want to hear from me.

- If they open it, they stay on the list. If not, I delete them. Note - I don't unsubscribe them, as it might keep them from signing up in the future. Just delete them.

That keeps the list clean and active. It raises my percentage of opens and clicks.

People are savvy these days. They know when someone is wasting their time with click-baity emails. So I always send something valuable and useful to them. And if they are too busy to unsubscribe, I do it for them. It's the idea of having 1,000 true fans, the ones that will open (and buy) anything you ask them to. A thousand hyper-active fans is worth as much as the 1% of a 10,000 name list who do. But you can mail to a thousand people for free, and pay a lot to mail to 10,000 each week.

Email hygiene saves you money and reputation.

> *PS. Out of a few hundred people who have been sent that "Still Interested?" email, only two ever complained. And in both cases, this was the first email they opened from me. Go figure. Their lives must be truly tough to get triggered so easily.*

- How to Mail Out Multiple Giveaways. Let your list decide what they want. I put up a site page entitled "Free Books" and list all the active giveaways on it. New ones close to the top. My own giveaways at the very top. (Right below my "featured books of the week.") Then my weekly newsletter - just to the people who came in from giveaways - goes out with a link to that page (and my latest release - both as bitly-shortened links.) I may be in 20 giveaways simultaneously. And several will have truly lousy graphics or none. But the best ones will attract the most, regardless of where they are on the page. Longer-running ones will eventually gravitate to the bottom. Update every week, usually on a Monday, and send it out. While maybe not as effective as just sending it to a single giveaway, it helps all of them a little bit. Bitly links show me how many clicks I got that went where. I customize the name on every bitly link so that I can see which giveaway it pointed to.

That fulfills any promise to "mail to your list".

- **Using Buffer to Do Social Media.** I'm no fan of social media. I'd rather be writing, publishing, or researching than having to wade through cat pictures and troll comments. I've spent hours with nothing to show for it, and so quit visiting ("engaging") at most of these platforms. I only work at syndicating my blog content out by automatic (using IFTTT.com.) I don't really care if anyone "follows" me. I use it more as a way to leverage all the valuable content I'm publishing otherwise (and I've gone over this many places on my LiveSensical.com site.) Buffer (and probably HootSuite) are good for simple sending out the same content to different platforms from a single interface. For me, this is Facebook, Twitter, G+. Not Instagram or Pinterest as those depend on different graphics going up with each post, while our use of social media is to promote giveaways (That have a single banner.) Sending once a day keeps you on the free Buffer account limits. (Since I always log out of Facebook when I leave them, using a 3rd-party app also limits the amount of data they can scrape from me.)

My approach is this:

- Don't "engage," syndicate.

- Use one interface only.

- Don't pay to use free platforms. ("If it's free, *you* are the product.")

- Uses of Pen Names and Imprints. I've seen a lot and tested a lot. And what I don't see many people using is pen names. I got this originally from a couple of sources, but Geoff Shaw recommends this for starting authors. Because you are going to be improving as you go, and if your early stuff might embarrass you later, then use another name. While Instafreebie allows you to have up to five pen names at their Pro level, most beginning authors are struggling to pay their lowest paid level of $20 per month. The work around for this is to have the name there be your publishing imprint (like "Midwest Journal Press") and then the individual books can be "[Title] by [Author]".

The trade off is that when other authors/imprints are giving you blurbs, they can only do one per account to another account. Having three or four books up by any given pen name will give you only one blurb for all the pen names you use under that imprint. No big deal, usually.

One advantage to the Pro Version is that I can submit books by all five pen names to that one giveaway, and they show up as separate entities. When I promote, the giveaway organizer sees my actual account name, which doesn't line up to any of the pen names. But again, I see very few people using pen names at all, let alone figuring out the "imprint" strategy.

One point here – when a giveaway is only opening it up to a limited amount of books. Some do as few as 10. So if you enter one book per each pen name, then you won't have 10 authors with 10 lists. You really will be responsible for half of the claims of that giveaway.

The overall advantage to pen names is using them to separate your genres. Also, the different universes/world-views you are writing in.

- Why "No Limits" Gets You More - Everything. I'm a great one for mastering the "firehose" approach to content. This extends to giveaways as well. The ones I hate to join are the "control freaks" who want to enforce that you do the giveaway their way or else. Sure, there are Leechers who don't actually promote the giveaway. And it might be that only 20% of all your authors are actually producing the claims. (Meaning that maybe 50% of the books up there are getting claims and being subscribed to for doing nothing.) But look at it this way: You're building great karma (and the others, well...)

The point of No Limits Approach is to help others as you'd like to be helped. Again, building karma open-handedly. The more restrictive you make your giveaway, the fewer people will join in on it. Of course, we always can't all just do Romance/Erotica or Fantasy/Science Fiction giveaways. That gets boring real quick. As you complete giveaways, you start building a track record of where your books have produced well. And that gives you an idea of what type of giveaways you want to mirror. And new combinations of genres and inspired themes you may want to try.

You'll also see that when a person limits their giveaways to just 10 or 30 books, they are limiting the amount of authors who can join. And so, are limited to the possible amount of people they can reach. Same goes for restrictive forms that "must" be filled out before your book can be "accepted." The more hoops you have to jump through, the less likely you are to do anything.

The inverse of this is to get over a hundred authors, some with several books into your list. Then that 20% will be 20 people sending to their lists and socials, not just 2.

This also applies to how long you set your giveaway into the future. If you only give people a couple of weeks, you might only have a few books. Give them a couple of months, and they'll trickle in and keep filling. The most successful giveaways I've been part of so far had well over a hundred books submitted. See how that works?

Just my opinion – based on natural laws that have been on the books since before writing was invented.

How to Mine Your Completed Giveaway

There's nothing better than mining (and finding) gold in your own back yard.

Instafreebie gives you tons of data from your completed giveaways. Not just the ones you've organized, but all of them.

What is key is to see how you could improve your claims. These days, especially since EU GDPR rules, your claims don't automatically translate into subscribers. But the more claims you have, the more possible subscribers can get.

There are lots of variables that seem to influence this:

• Mostly, your cover and description. Going through the books that were part of that giveaway can give you examples of what to do and not to do.

• What genre may have something to do with it.

• How many authors or participants also can have an effect, as each author has their own mailing list and social media followers.

• How many books each author has in the giveaway may give them a larger piece of the giveaway pie. Different books attract different readers.

• How long the giveaway is open might affect the total number of claims.

After a few months, you'll have several giveaways available as data in your Instafreebie account. These are listed as "completed." In those files, you'll see all the claims for every book, a total for the giveaway, and dates. You also have access to all the comments that were left (including any links people have given out.)

I took the first two months of the giveaways I've been part of and dropped them into a spreadsheet for data mining. (The original article and trying to reproducing it in a book tends to trash the presentation, though. Access here: https://calm.li/CompletedGiveawaysSheet)

Let's review those variables again: If you suse the shared file[1] you can re-sort them for yourself. The default presented is sorted by Average Claim Per Book, as it seems to give the most direct correlations.

1. *Cover and description aren't available on this spreadsheet.* You will be able to see which giveaways need more study, though.
2. *Genre might be a factor.* You can see that Cosy Mystery is at the top, but Contemporary Romance holds the next two spots. There are other Romance combinations showing up lower. Non-Fiction is at the bottom. It may mean our sample is too small.
3. While *more authors might make for more discovery*, and certainly the highest number of claims on this list had the most authors, it also diluted the numbers of claims per book. This might argue for a limited number authors/books. Average on this list of giveaways was 53 books.
4. *The length of the giveaway didn't seem to have any noticeable effect.* The average length on this small spreadsheet is 15 days, and most are around two-three weeks. Again, we need more data here. One IF support person told me the most common is a month, but I don't see that here. Still, I've set up several month-long giveaways which will complete by the end of this year. Also, I've set up some 10-day "blitz" giveaways that are only Sun - Tues so I can possibly get them featured on Instafreebie's mailings and website. We'll see.

Other factors:

• *Several authors have as many as seven or more books in each giveaway.* This doesn't show in the spreadsheet above. But in averaging these out on a couple of giveaways, it did show that the number of books was still just over one book per author. Still, this gives an idea to have multiple books in each giveaway.

---

1. https://calm.li/CompletedGiveawaysSheet

• *Another is whether other giveaways are running for the same genre.* These overlap all over the place, regardless of genre, and the biggest claim totals were among those with other conflicts. This seems to point to the most engaged authors with the biggest lists. Again, we need a larger sample, and more data available as an organizer.

• *Private giveaways aren't part of this dataset.* That will be as you can build a network of authors, generally by running giveaways so you can see who are the ones that really contribute and do well. (You might find these authors by claiming their books and getting on their mailing lists yourself...)

Some preliminary conclusions:

• **More books are better** - bigger piece of the total claims for any giveaway. A better chance that the reader will like at least one of your books more than the others.

• **More giveaways are better**. "The more times you enter the greater chances of winning."

• **Organize and run giveaways yourself, constantly.**

• **It mostly matters that you enter giveaways and contribute to them by promoting** to whatever list and social media that you have. (Build good Karma by contributing.)

Additional: If you download your subscribers and sort them by giveaway and book, then you'll also start seeing a pattern of which of these completed giveaways was the most productive for you. Just cross-compare these two spreadsheets and you'll have tons of data.

Visiting the completed giveaways to check which were the most-claimed books will tell you about your artwork and description as well...

Marketing Plans

I had to write this chapter before I could outline the few action steps (in its own chapter) that seem obvious at this point.

You use Instafreebie as another tool in your Marketing toolbox.

Marketing is just part of building your author platform.

Regardless of what others say, *your platform is your business.* It's not just about selling books. There's a natural system in place that is growing or shrinking depending on your actions.

The other point you have to know is that marketing by definition is *the action of finding and building a market.* A market it a place (actual or virtual) for exchanging your valuable goods (completed product or services) for someone else's commodity called money.

Promotion isn't marketing, it's just part of it. Promotion is getting in front of someone else's audience and getting them to join yours. Back from that you want both the audience-handler's permission and recommendation. You are giving something of value so that the audience will then opt-in to yours, with the idea of getting more value in the future.

Paid ads are simply your paying to get access to someone else's audience. Advertising is a small part of promotion. There are many, many more ways to promote than that.

Instafreebie has a large list of people it mails to. By joining Instafreebie (especially the paid versions) you are getting permission to talk to their audience. Getting subscribers is a method of enabling their audience to join yours.

What you are interested in is subscribers that actually open your emails and click on your links. Just because you have subscribers doesn't mean that you have anything.

The real marketing is to turn these subscribers into regular fans. Buying fans. Fans that leave reviews (on Amazon, anyway.) Fans that recommend your book to other fans, especially Avid Readers. Fans that will also buy your non-fiction books and courses. Fans that become evangelists (and affiliates) for your books, products, and services.

That is marketing.

How easy this can be depends on how well you've grown your platform.

Four Parts to Your Author Platform.

There are four parts. And I credit Tim Grahl for showing me three of them (well, 2 ½.)

1. **Value** – your Content

2. **Audience** – Subscribers

3. **Network** – Authors you can work with.

4. **Bliss** – What you like to do most, what brings you the most joy.

These are all integrated as a system, and as you grow one point, you'll grow the rest.

In Instafreebie, you can build two of these – Audience and Network. Unstated is the quality of your ebooks (content) that you are including, and whether you really like writing in those genres and entertaining readers. But those other two points have to be there for you to be a success.

- You provide books to download for free. (Content.)

- Readers download these and join your list. (Audience.)

- You put out forms to collect author emails. (Network.)

- And you have fun at this, not just make it into another Job. (Bliss.)

As you then convert your subscribers to buying readers, then you'll build your market. That is marketing.

And email is the most effective way to market (and always has been.)

Buying access to audience is cheapest on Instafreebie, although Wattpad, and Medium are probably close runners-up. Way more expensive are Facebook and Amazon ads, where you can blow through money quickly with no result unless you watch those egg-baskets closely.

I'm a champion of making your author platform (business) pay for itself as it grows. Putting books up and sending more people to buy them makes a lot of sense. Books are themselves lead generators. But I'm still watching to make Instafreebie pay the investment I've made in it, other than being the cheapest way to "buy" subscribers. Those subscribers need to buy in turn.

It's always been any marketer's job to turn leads into paying customers and regular clients – fans. Then turn those fans into evangelists.

Those steps are all how you apply the four points of your author platform and make them grow.

Prolific or Single-Book Author?

This isn't a black and white scene.

Some people literally have only a single book in them. And that book needs to be brought to life and allowed to live.

Other people can access an unending flow of stories. Their job is to be midwife to birthing hundreds of stories, short and long. Helping them all to live out in the world of published books.

A small handful of these will live forever as perennially-selling books. This is the holy grail of authors. To have their book or some of their books be on sale all the time. Louis L'Amour was a more modern version of Shakespeare. Both have books that simply don't go out of print and are continually in demand. Other authors have done this. Some, like Herman Melville and Henry David Thoreau, did this posthumously.

A modern author (like J. K. Rowling, Hugh Howey, James Patterson) would prefer to have this happen in their own lifetime.

Most of these authors have a series of books that they promote and market to accomplish this. Or they get someone to do those actions for them.

Prolific is always a choice. You can grow into this.

And prolific is a way to beat the Amazon algorithms and start making an actual viable income from their writing. Prolific authors promote their earlier books by having new books promote their backlist.

Others have make a living from their books by running consistent and continuing promotional campaigns on their few books.

Both approaches work.

And once you have that audience, that network, that platform – you then can extend your brand into courses and additional materials. (See Mark Dawson and Nick Stephenson as fiction author-examples, Tim Grahl and his clients as nonfiction author-examples.)

All of this is how you build your marketing.

Action Steps

1. Ensure you are happy writing and promoting what you write.
2. Get a handful of books (they can be previews or short stories) in every genre you write in.
3. Get these up on Instafreebie using their existing covers and descriptions. (You can come back and improve these later.)
4. Join a few giveaways to get the hang of how they work.
5. Organize a few giveaways to get the hang of how they work.
6. Set up a schedule to deal with the Instafreebie emails and also the maintenance you have to do in running giveaways.
7. Once you can deal with the flood of traffic, enter all possible giveaways with your existing books, making sure that you actually do promote every single giveaway somehow.
8. Set up a regular set of giveaways so that you always have one of your own organized giveaways running.
9. Start aggregating author emails to coordinate your giveaways with them. Help them every way you can to achieve their own success.
10. Based on data-mining your completed giveaways and your subscriber lists, streamline which genres are more effective for you to promote and what books are your best lead generators.
11. Adjust your giveaways accordingly.
12. Regularly review your data to look for seasonal trends. Tweak everything against best results.
13. Always work for the long view, the long haul. Iterate.
14. Test your results against your own satisfaction and those of your audience and your network.

Supplement

(Expect this area to grow in later editions...)

A Rough Idea of How to Get Everything Done

My Instafreebie emails dropped off the last few days, meaning that people haven't commented on anything recently and there haven't been a lot of new giveaways announced. (Or I've just gotten more efficient...)

This means I have time to organize a bit better – and so this figure-out added just before I finalize this book for publishing.

The main point of organizing is to allot some time daily to keep up with things. Instafreebie doesn't have to take a lot of time daily or weekly to keep on top of things. But having at least a loose schedule could help.

1. **Handle your Instafreebie emails daily,** during the time you normally check emails. I find that I can handle approving/rejecting new submissions with my smartphone, and so do this after meals each day. Comments emails are more of the read-and-archive variety. (Thankfully, there isn't a huge social aspect to this site.)

2. **Weekly** - Take your best performing books and look for more places to put them. I've found that I don't necessarily seem to get all the new giveaways (or my email is hiding them from me.) So it's good to go through all the giveaways and enter the ones you feel you can with books that are appropriate. Once a week should do you.

3. **Also weekly** - a couple of days later, you'll have books approved. Now is the time to go back through and update all your exclusive ones so they stand out. You have to check each book one by one. The most recent ones are on top, so you don't have to check all of them again. Once a week should be fine.

4. **Mon/Wed/Fri?** For any giveaway you've organized, I'd suggest giving an at-taboy or helpful tip as a comment every other day or so. This was rarely done in the ones I've participated in. But the more interaction you do, the more Instafree-

bie will smile on giving you a Verified Status. (And that will make it possible to get even more subscribers...) So: three times a week or so.

5. **Tuesdays or when your giveaways end** – Now is the time for the Big Push to get everyone to send out for the final days of the giveaway. This is also when a lot of claims happen. Just human nature. And the old phrase, "You Can't Get the Sale You Don't Ask For" also applies to claims and subscriptions. At least they can send out to social media if they don't want to nag their email list.

6. **When any giveaway ends** – make sure you send out a link in the comments to your authors to join your list by filling out that Google form. That also applies to any giveaway you haven't organized. This is obviously another service you can provide in order to network with others.

7. **After your giveaway ends** – *Updating A/B descriptions:* If you have a clear winner, then update your description with the new one. Also send out the winning description to anyone you've been running A/B tests for.

8. **Once Monthly Analysis** – analyze your subscribers to find the best performing books and giveaways. Probably right at the tend of the month, as a lot of giveaways run for a whole calendar month. Also follow up with which covers and descriptions performed best for those top giveaways. So that's three analyses (although you can put them all on a spreadsheet for that month by adding more pages to the spreadsheet in tabs:

- Your total subscribers list is the base. This is going to get huge after awhile, so you might want to narrow this down to just that month's completed giveaways.

- That month's list of completed giveways, their dates, genres, and total claims.

- A review of the top-claimed books in the completed giveaways by cover image and description.

At the end of that review, organize any additional giveaways you need according to what giveaways are available for your genres.

Final Notes

This book is a continuing work in progress. I'll revise this as I can to keep it accurate and up-to-date

If you have questions, or see an error, you can always contact me. I answer all emails as long as they aren't scams or spam. Just real folks with real questions.

Join my list and you'll have my email address. Simple.

Use this link: https://calm.li/InstafreebieAuthors

The one above is for Instafreebie Authors. If you just want my free books, then...

Use this link: https://calm.li/MidwestJournalPressGiveaways

Don't miss out!

Click the button below and you can sign up to receive emails whenever Dr. Robert C. Worstell publishes a new book. There's no charge and no obligation.

https://books2read.com/r/B-A-GDXD-ZTXS

BOOKS 2 READ

Connecting independent readers to independent writers.

Did you love *A Completely Unauthorized Instafreebie Guidebook*? Then you should read *Author Freedom Guidebook* by Dr. Robert C. Worstell!

Your writing and publishing should give you freedom.

And for most people, it doesn't.

Because only four out of ten thousand authors actually make a living by publishing through Amazon.

Shocking statistics.

As a writer, the solution is simple: learn how the system works. Then do that.

After five years of concentrated research, I've narrowed down to exactly what the core basics are that most authors have been missing.

There have been a few breakthroughs:

What actually is a platform - and how you already have one.

The three habits you have to have in order to succeed.

Four steps you need to do before you start writing or outlining your book.

The two biggest lies spread in publishing.

How you can teach yourself to write classic bestsellers at home.

The biggest revelation is that, like Dorothy's ruby slippers, you already know most of this. The problem is that you've been trained not to believe it.

This book is also a course. In 7 simple lessons, you can get started now toward a full-time career as a successful author.

It won't happen overnight. But you'll be on your way.

Success is waiting for you, along with your freedom.

Get Your Copy Now.

Online course and additional materials are available at http://livesensical.com/go/author-freedom/

Also by Dr. Robert C. Worstell

Make Yourself Great Again Library
Why You Got All That Stuff
The Art of Wonk, Compleat

Mindset Stacking Guides
Make Yourself Great Again Part 1
Make Yourself Great Again Part 2
Make Yourself Great Again Part 3
Make Yourself Great Again Part 4
Choose. Believe. Win.
Make Yourself Great Again - Complete Collection

Really Simple Writing & Publishing
How To Write And Publish For Free
Backwards Book Publishing: Save Time, Earn More, Work Less
Writing-Publishing Survival Guide
Author Freedom Guidebook
How to Stop Feeding the Beast
A Completely Unauthorized Instafreebie Guidebook